Boo

IN RECITAL®
WITH POPULAR CHRISTMAS MUSIC

ABOUT THE SERIES • A NOTE TO THE TEACHER

In Recital® *with Popular Christmas Music* is devoted to fabulous Christmas repertoire. The two outstanding composers/arrangers of this series, Edwin McLean and Kevin Olson, have created engaging arrangements of timeless Christmas pieces, which have been carefully leveled to ensure success with this repertoire. We know that to motivate, the teacher must challenge the student with attainable goals. This series makes that possible while also providing a perfect holiday treat for your students. You will find favorites that are easy to sing along with as well as recital-style arrangements. You will also find two new Christmas gems by the composers! This series complements other FJH publications, and will help you plan student recital repertoire for holiday season recitals. The books include CDs with complete performances designed to assist with recital preparation. Throughout this series you will find interesting background information for each Christmas piece by Dave Olsen.

Use the enclosed CD as a teaching and motivational tool. For a guide to listening to the CD, turn to page 39.

Production: Frank J. Hackinson
Production Coordinators: Joyce Loke and Satish Bhakta
Cover Art Concept: Helen Marlais
Cover Design: Terpstra Design, San Francisco, CA
Cover Illustration: Sophie Library
Engraving: Tempo Music Press, Inc.
Printer: Tempo Music Press, Inc.

ISBN-13: 978-1-56939-726-8

ORGANIZATION OF THE SERIES
IN RECITAL® WITH POPULAR CHRISTMAS MUSIC

The series is carefully leveled into the following six categories: Early Elementary, Elementary, Late Elementary, Early Intermediate, Intermediate, and Late Intermediate. Each of the works has been selected for its artistic as well as its pedagogical merit.

Book One — Early Elementary, reinforces the following concepts:

- Basic notes such as quarter, half, dotted half, and whole notes are used.

- $\frac{3}{4}$ and $\frac{4}{4}$ time signatures are used.

- Students play with a detached as well as a smooth touch.

- Most of the pieces call for limited use of hands-together playing.

- Pieces reinforce basic musical terminology and symbols such as *forte, piano, mezzo forte, mezzo piano,* repeat signs, tied notes, and *fermata.*

- Pieces use middle C as well as other basic hand positions.

- Basic Keys—C major, G major, and F major (written using accidentals instead of key signatures).

Many of the solos in Book One have teacher accompaniments to enhance the overall sound of the piece. The solos, however, stand on their own as recital pieces.

TABLE OF CONTENTS

FJH1761

ABOUT THE PIECES AND COMPOSERS

Good King Wenceslas

Good King Wenceslas was indeed a real person. He lived in the tenth century, but he wasn't a king. He was the Duke of Bohemia, a land presently within the borders of the Czech Republic in Europe, and his name wasn't Wenceslas. It was Vaclav. As the song suggests, he was a very kind man and was eventually named the patron saint of his native land. The music for this piece originated in the sixteenth century and was a Latin carol known as *Tempus adest floridum* (Spring has now unwrapped the flowers). It was England's John Mason Neale, who, in the mid-1800s, put the story of the kindly Duke Vaclav together with this sprightly melody.

Go, Tell It On the Mountain

Go, Tell It On the Mountain is an African-American spiritual that dates back to around 1865. The original composer is not known, but some attribute the song to a noted Nashville-based composer, scholar Frederick J. Work. This energetic piece has been sung and recorded by many gospel and secular performers. It is considered a Christmas carol because its original lyric celebrates the Nativity.

Sweet Little Jesus Boy

Robert MacGimsey's tender lullaby was written on Christmas Eve of 1932 and originally published as an "art song"—a song written for solo voice and accompaniment and intended for concert performance. While it is often performed by opera singers and performers in this music genre, it has also been recorded by artists such as Michael Jackson, country sensation Trisha Yearwood, and jazz great Nancy Wilson. This song is typically classified as a "spiritual." What type of song do you think it is?

ABOUT THE PIECES AND COMPOSERS

Christmas Is Coming

There are several different melodies associated with the lighthearted lyric of this holiday favorite. The version included in this book is perhaps the best known and was penned by English composer Edith Nesbit Bland. The form of this song is known as a "round"—a musical composition where multiple performers sing or play the same melody over and over again, with each starting at a different time. *Row, Row, Row Your Boat* is an example of a well-known round.

Do You Hear What I Hear?

This beautiful song was written by Noel Regney, a Frenchman trained as a classical composer, and Gloria Shayne. They met while Gloria was working as a pianist in a New York City hotel dining room and they married a month later. They wrote *Do You Hear What I Hear?* in 1962 during the Cuban Missile Crisis. While it is often taken for a Christmas carol, for Regney and Shayne this song is a hymn to peace. "Pray for peace, people everywhere."

A Merry Merry Christmas to You

Here's another delightful Christmas favorite in $\frac{3}{4}$ time by the writer of *Rudolph the Red-Nosed Reindeer*, Johnny Marks! His wish for everyone is that "each day be very, very happy all the year through." He also says that everyone will see various things that the Christmas spirit can do—bells ringing and people singing. Can you think of other things that the Christmas spirit makes you do?

Good King Wenceslas

Music: Traditional   Lyrics by John Mason Neale
arr. Edwin McLean

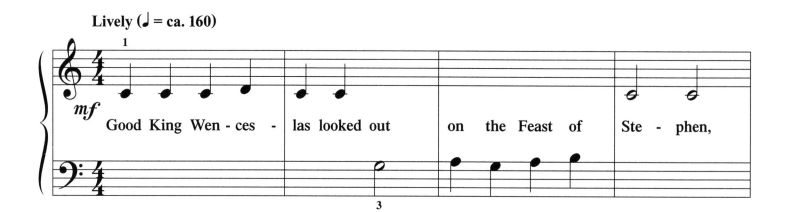

Good King Wen - ces - las looked out   on   the Feast of   Ste - phen,

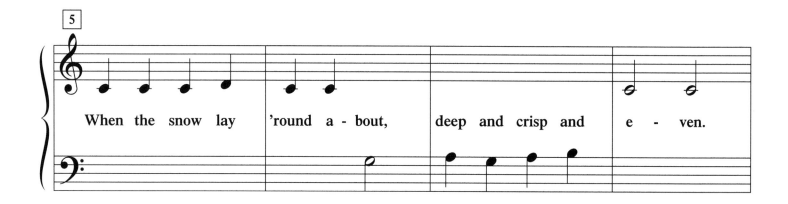

When the snow lay 'round a - bout,   deep and crisp and   e - ven.

Teacher Accompaniment: (*Student plays as written*)

L.H. only

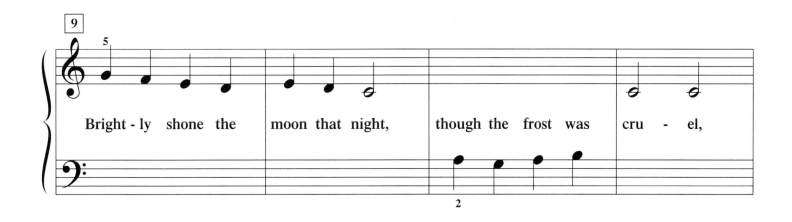

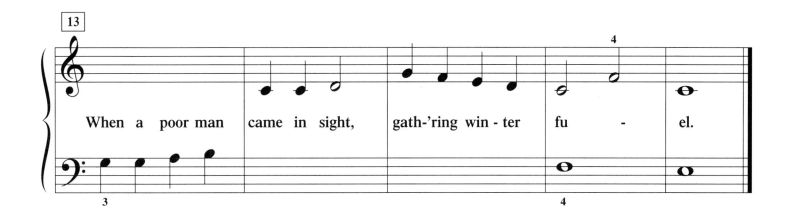

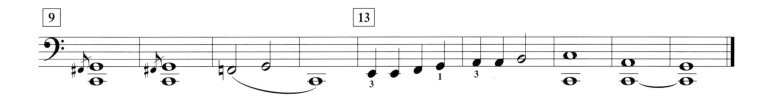

FJH1761

Go, Tell It On the Mountain

African-American Spiritual   arr. Edwin McLean

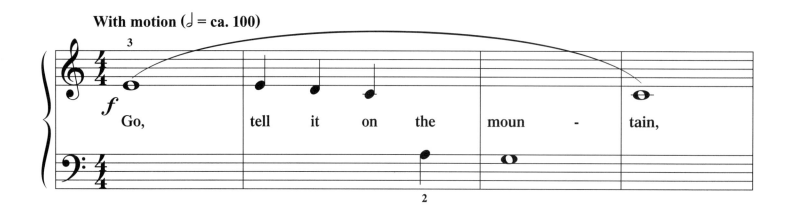

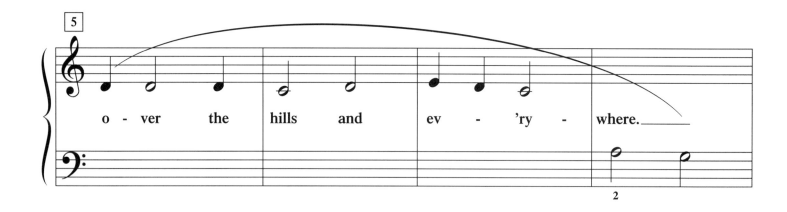

Teacher Accompaniment: *(Student plays one octave higher)*

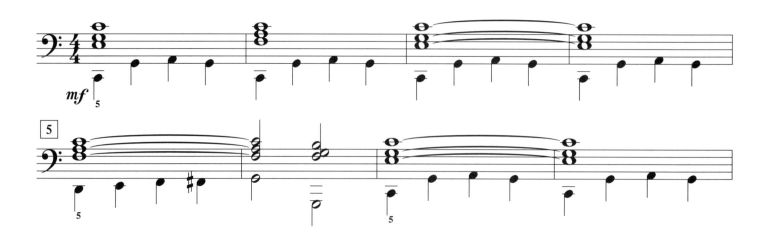

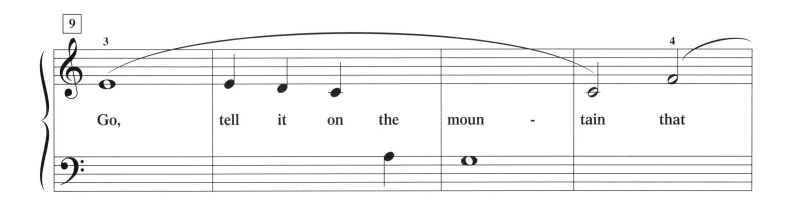

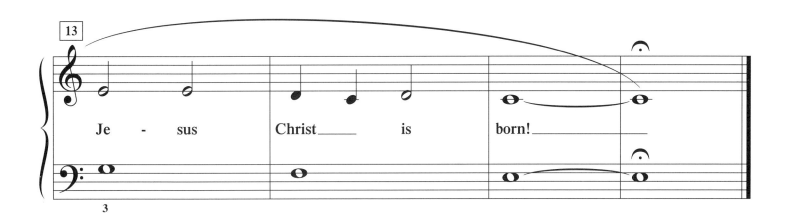

Sweet Little Jesus Boy

Music and Lyrics by Robert MacGimsey   arr. Kevin Olson

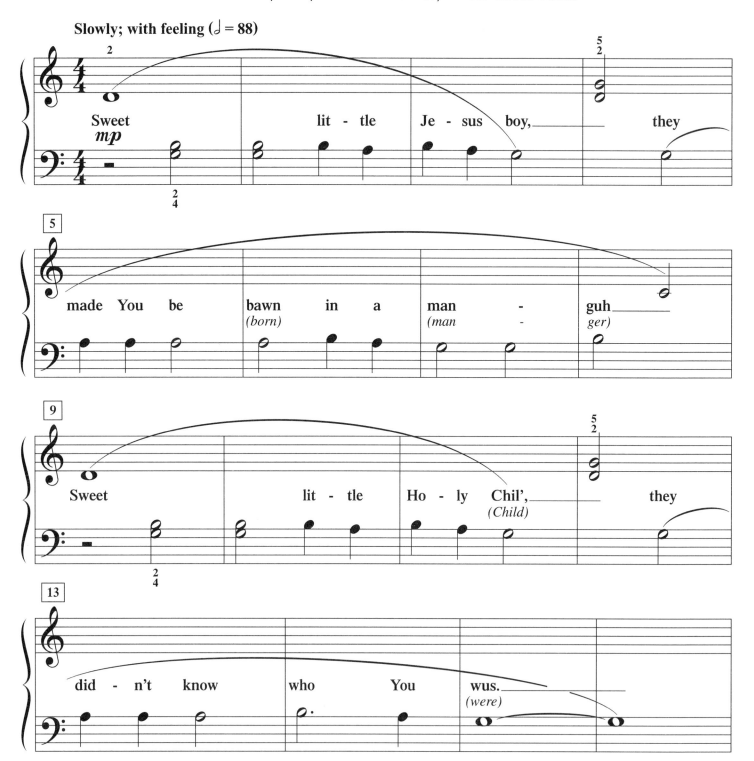

Lyrics under the staves:
Sweet   lit - tle   Je - sus boy,_____ they
made You be   bawn *(born)*   in a   man *(man* -   guh *ger)*_____
Sweet   lit - tle   Ho - ly Chil', *(Child)*_____ they
did - n't know   who   You   wus. *(were)*

Teacher Accompaniment: *(Student plays one octave higher)*

p
*legato
with pedal*

CHRISTMAS IS COMING

Music and Lyrics by Edith Nesbit Bland   arr. Kevin Olson

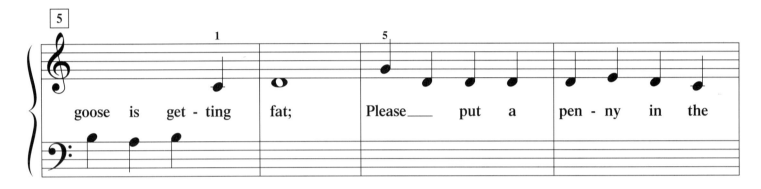

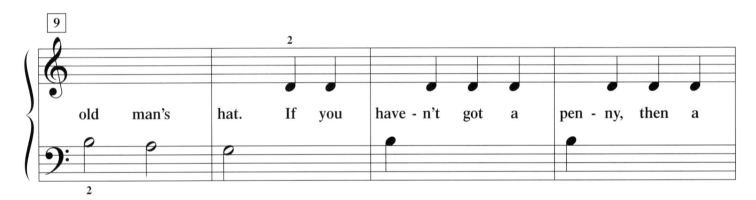

Teacher Accompaniment: (*Student plays one octave higher*)

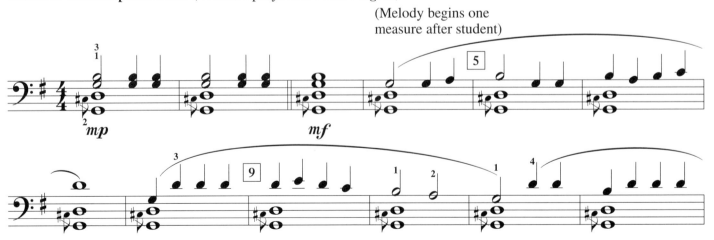

ha' - pen - ny will do; If you have - n't got a

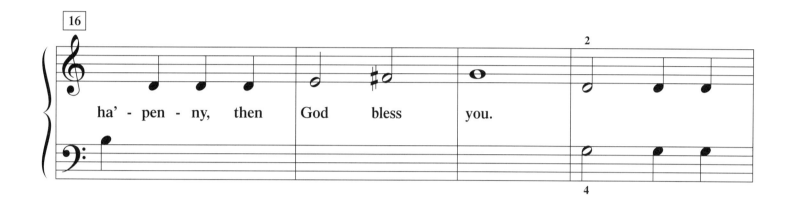

ha' - pen - ny, then God bless you.

gradually slowing down and becoming quieter

p

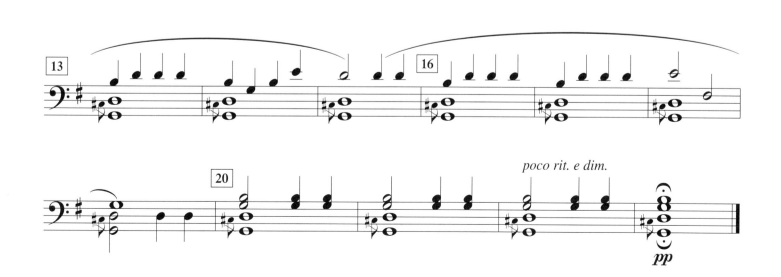

poco rit. e dim.

pp

Do You Hear What I Hear?

Music and Lyrics by Noel Regney and Gloria Shayne   arr. Kevin Olson

With majesty (♩ = ca. 168)

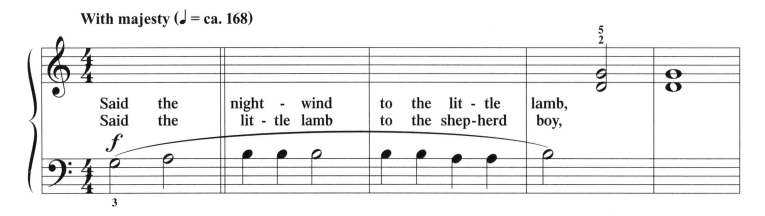

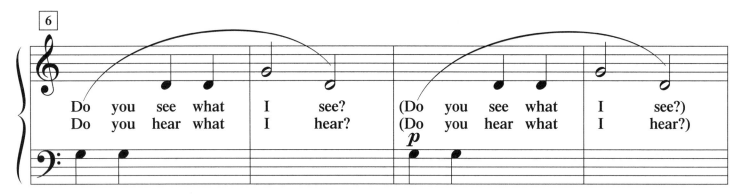

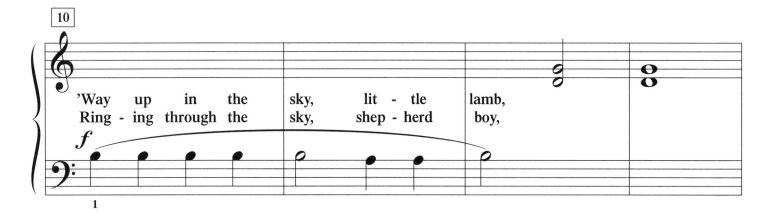

Teacher Accompaniment: (*Student plays as written*)

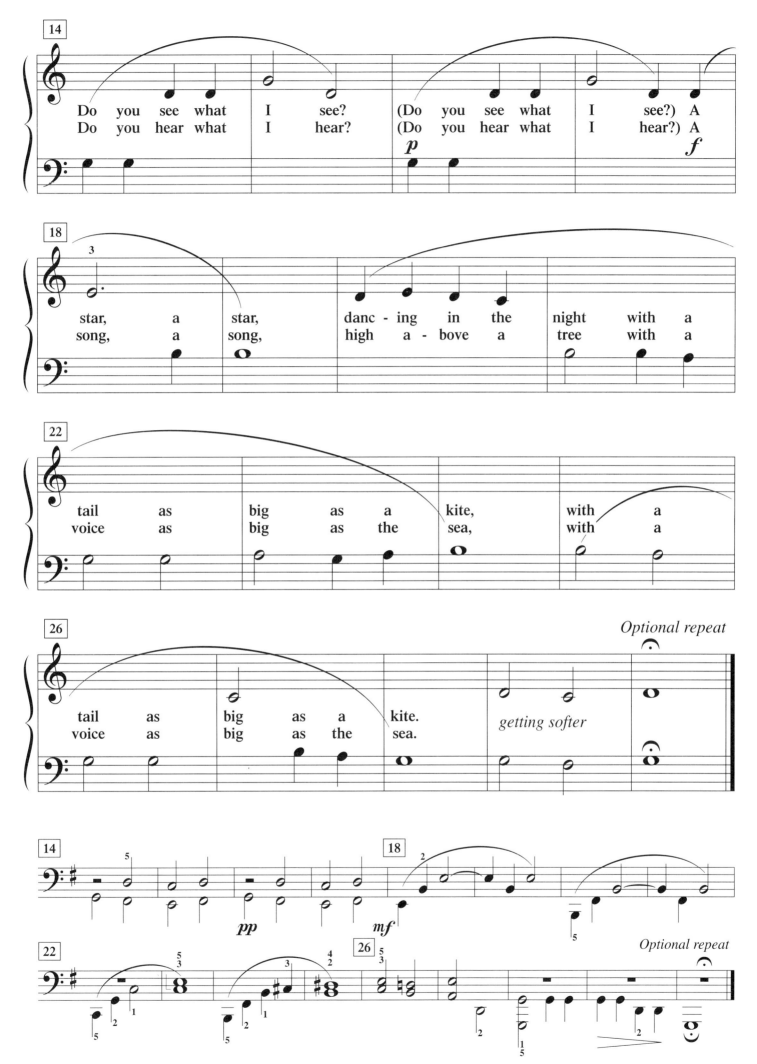

A MERRY MERRY CHRISTMAS TO YOU

Music and Lyrics by Johnny Marks   arr. Edwin McLean

With spirit! ($\downarrow$. = 66)

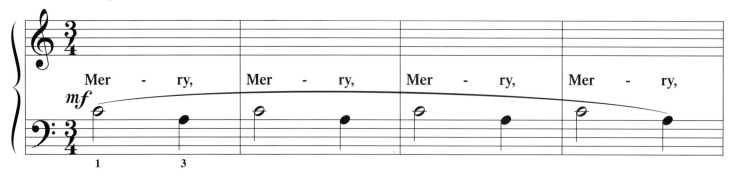

Mer - ry, Mer - ry, Mer - ry, Mer - ry,

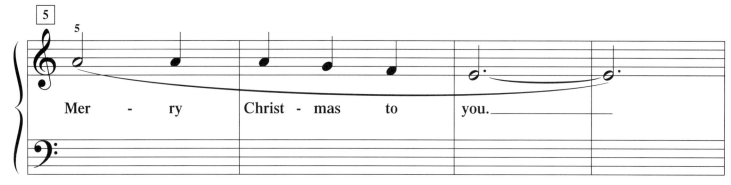

Mer - ry Christ - mas to you. _____

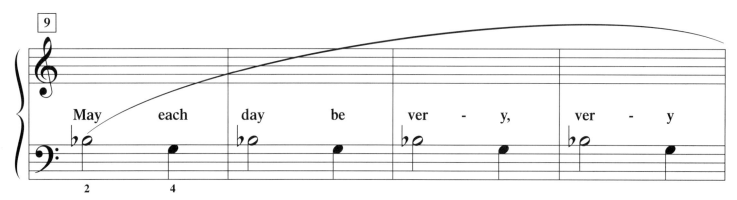

May each day be ver - y, ver - y

Teacher Accompaniment: *(Student plays one octave higher)*

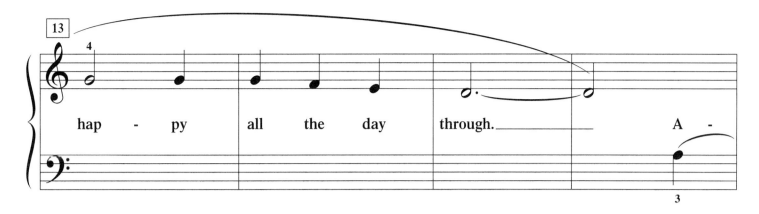

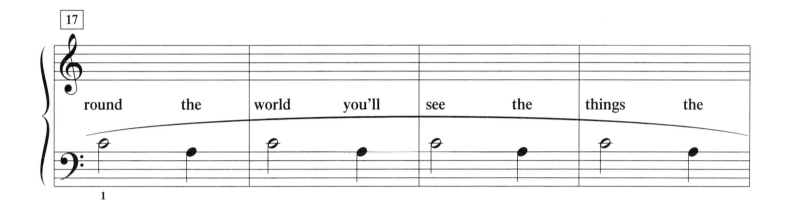

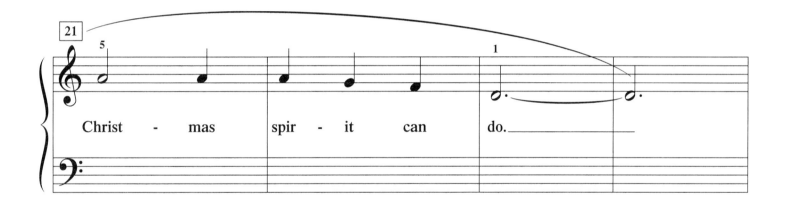

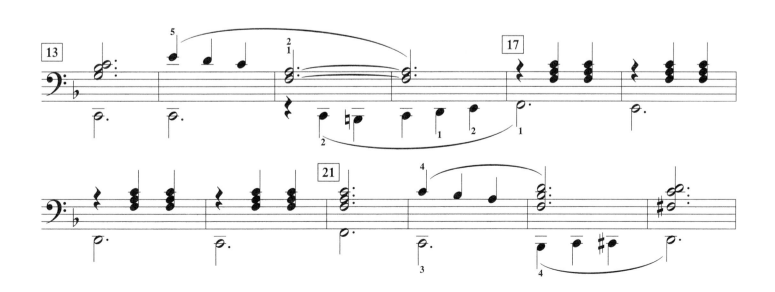

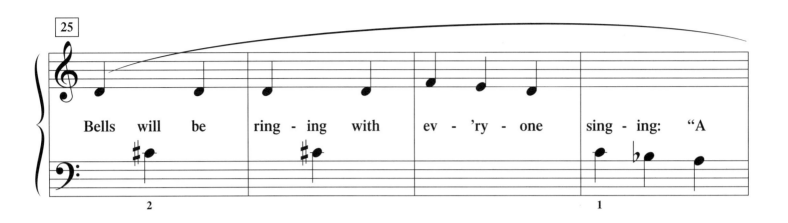

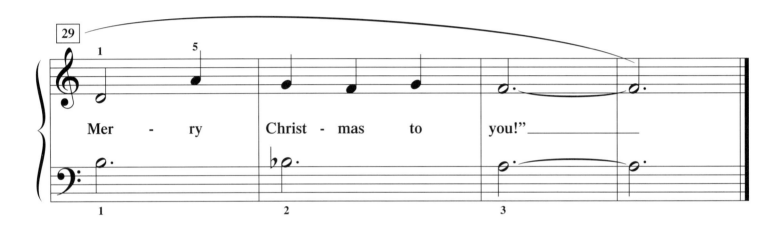

Santa Claus Is Comin' to Town

Music and Lyrics by J. Fred Coots and Haven Gillespie   arr. Kevin Olson

Lively, in two ($\quad$ = ca. 120)

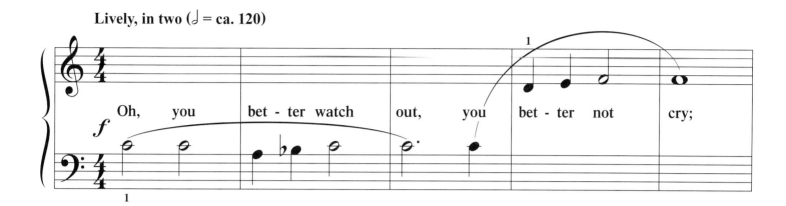

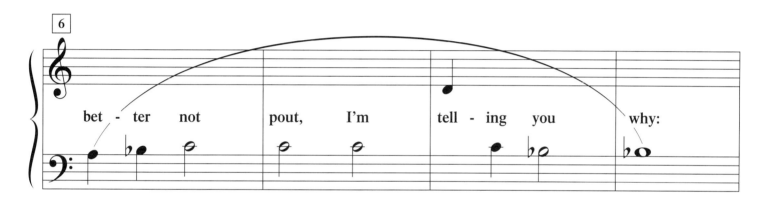

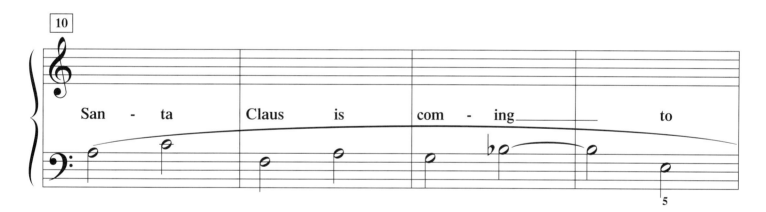

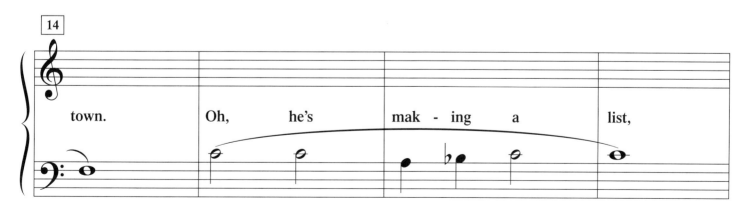

FJH1761

20

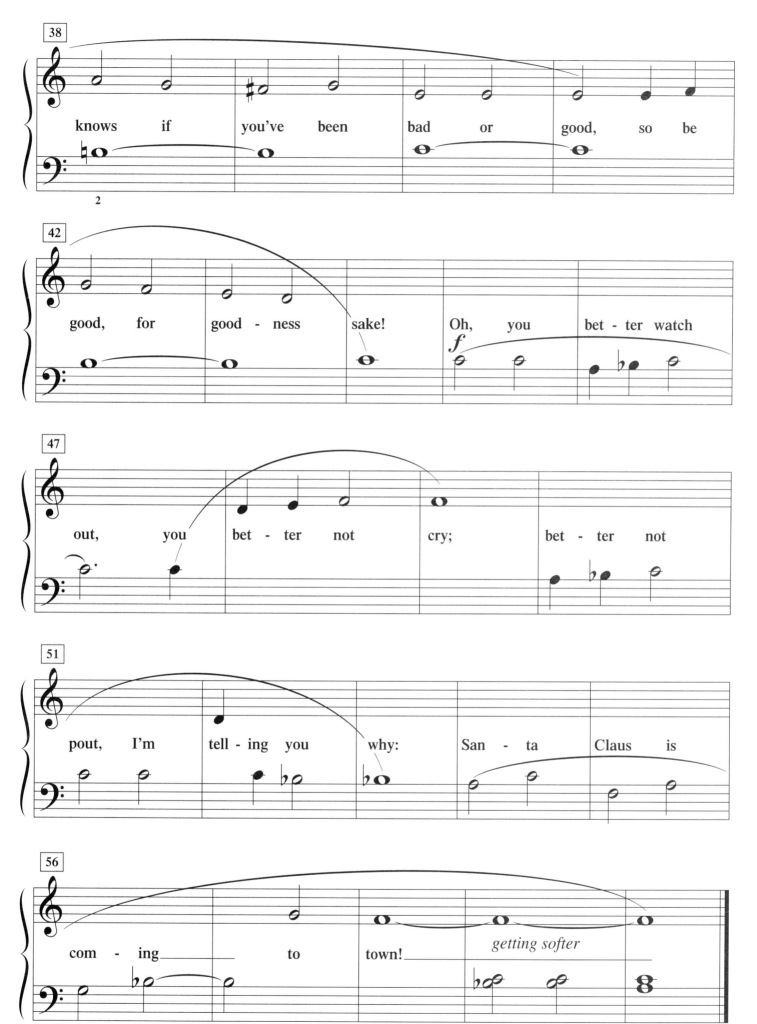

21

knows if you've been bad or good, so be

good, for good - ness sake! Oh, you bet - ter watch

out, you bet - ter not cry; bet - ter not

pout, I'm tell - ing you why: San - ta Claus is

com - ing to town! *getting softer*

FJH1761

(There's No Place Like) Home for the Holidays

Music and Lyrics by Al Stillman and Robert Allen   arr. Edwin McLean

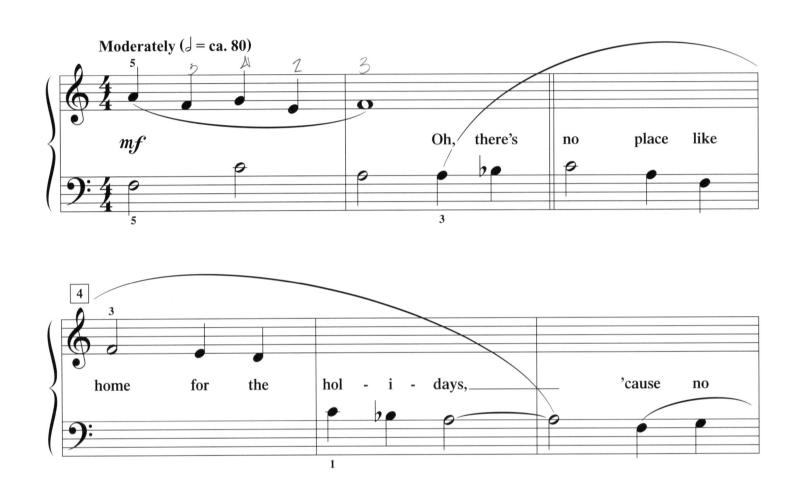

Teacher Accompaniment: *(Student plays one octave higher)*

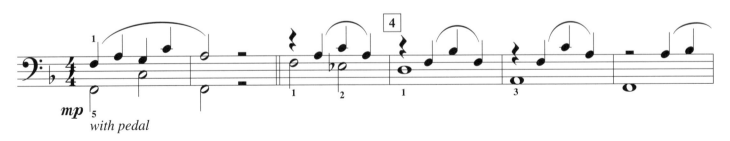

with pedal

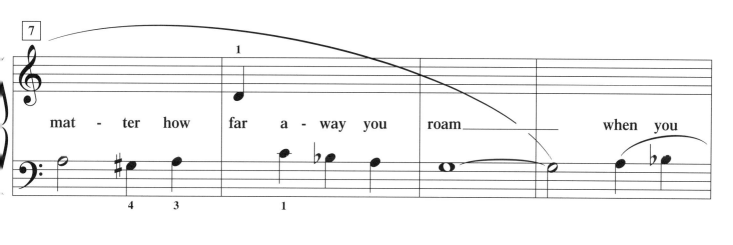

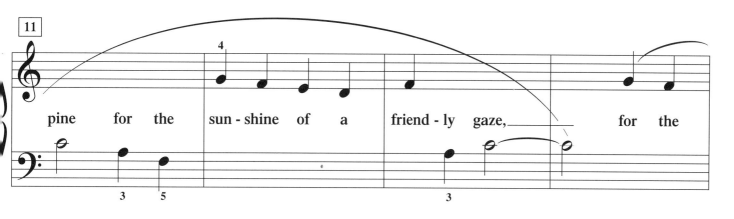

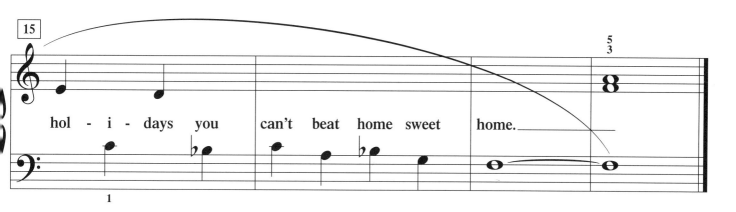

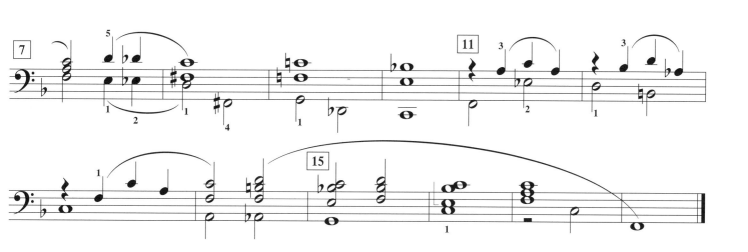

HE IS BORN

(Il est né)

Old French Carol   arr. Kevin Olson

Moderately ($\bullet$ = ca. 108)

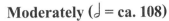

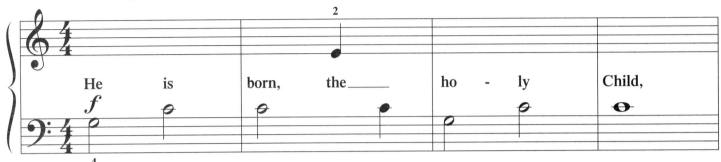

He is born, the_____ ho - ly Child,

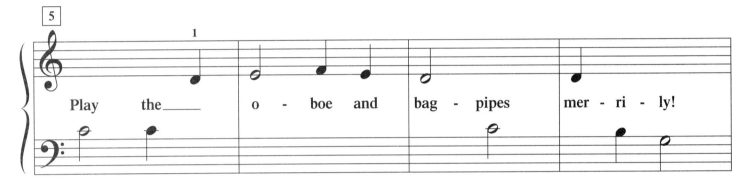

Play the_____ o - boe and bag - pipes mer - ri - ly!

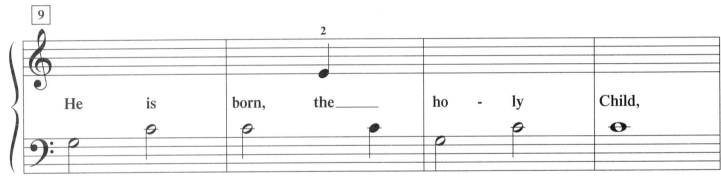

He is born, the_____ ho - ly Child,

Stop here after the 2nd time. (Fine)

Sing we_____ all to the Sav - ior mild.

Teacher Accompaniment: (*Student plays as written*)

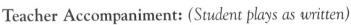

FJH1761

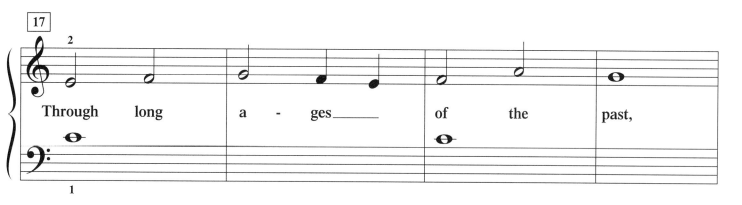

Through long a - ges____ of the past,

Proph - ets have fore - told His com - ing;

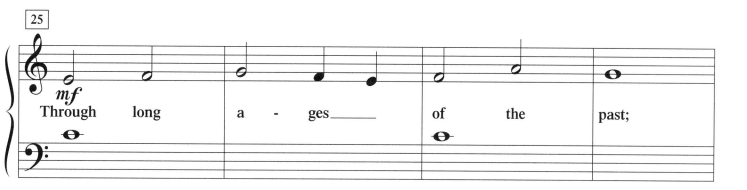

mf
Through long a - ges____ of the past;

*Go back to the beginning
and play the first four lines.*

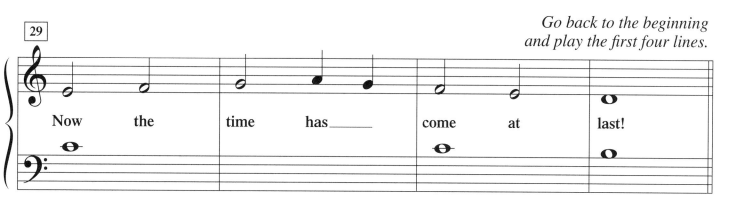

Now the time has____ come at last!

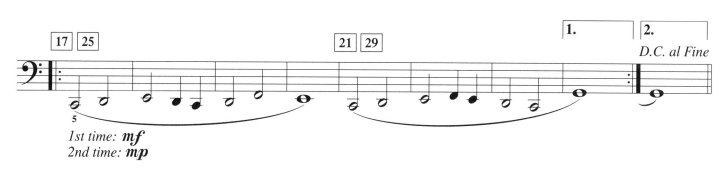

1st time: *mf*
2nd time: *mp*

D.C. al Fine

FJH1761

RUDOLPH THE RED-NOSED REINDEER

Music and Lyrics by Johnny Marks   arr. Kevin Olson

Teacher Accompaniment: (*Student plays one octave higher*)

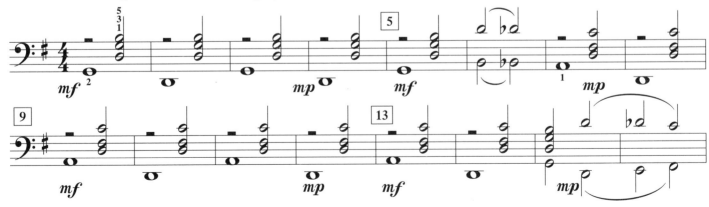

Then one fog - gy Christ - mas Eve

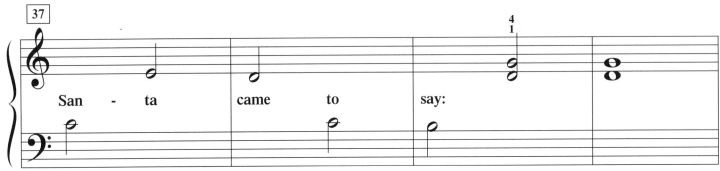

San - ta came to say:

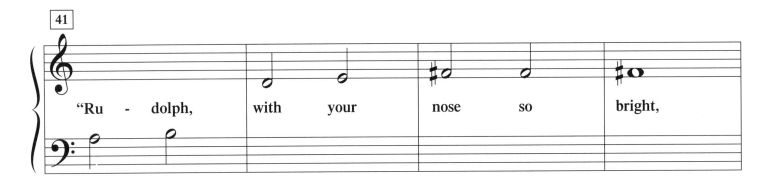

"Ru - dolph, with your nose so bright,

get louder
won't you guide my sleigh to - night?"

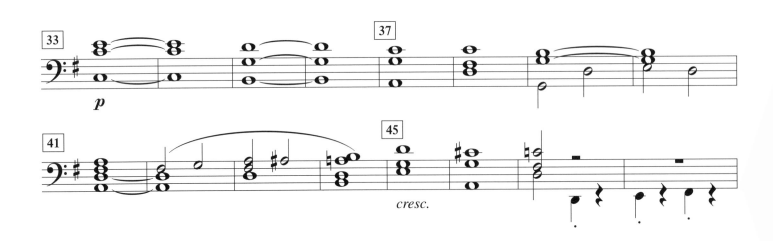

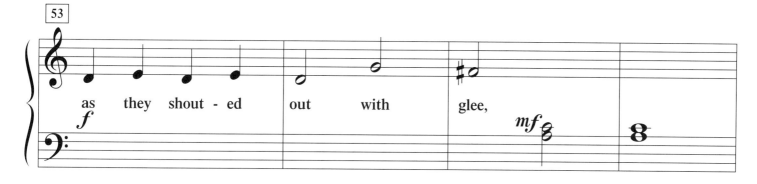

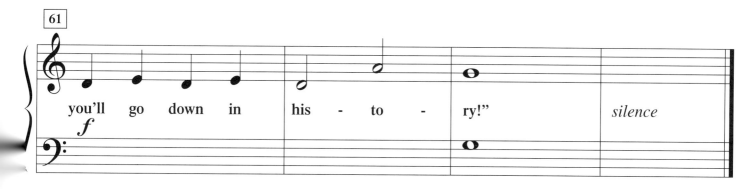

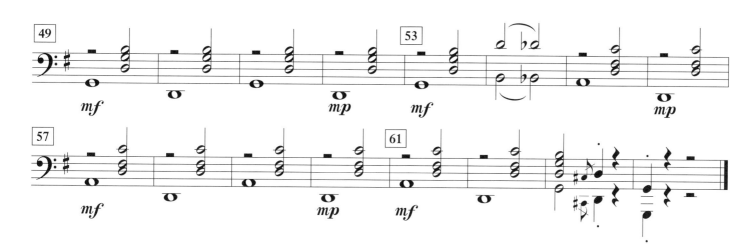

Over the River and Through the Woods

Music: Traditional   Lyrics by Lydia Maria Child   arr. Edwin McLean

DING DONG! MERRILY ON HIGH

Music: French Folk Melody Lyrics by George Ratcliffe Woodward
arr. Edwin McLean

Lively, in two (♩ = 100–120)

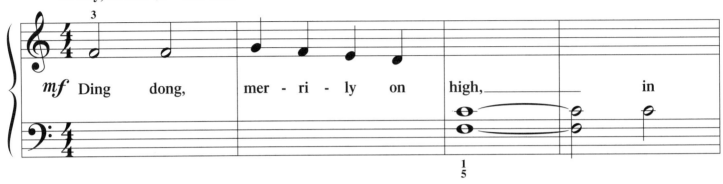

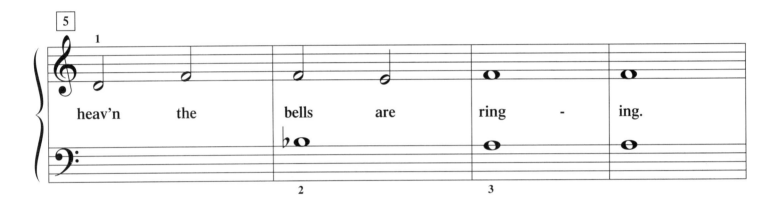

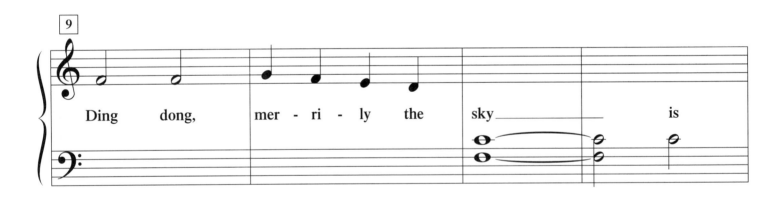

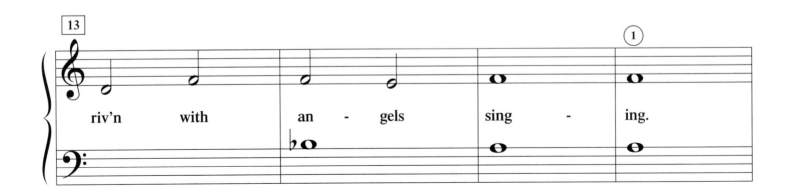

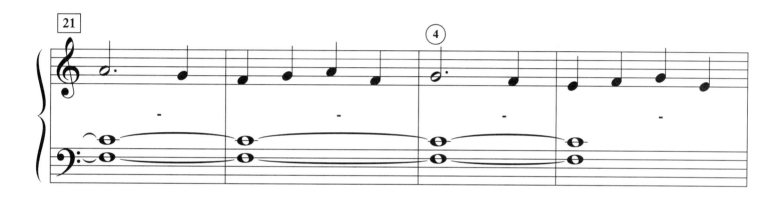

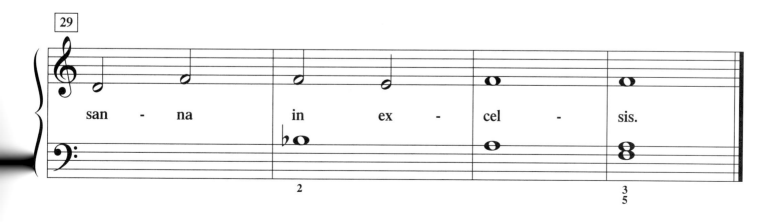

It's the Most Wonderful Time of the Year

Music and Lyrics by Edward Pola and George Wyle   arr. Edwin McLean

Teacher Accompaniment: *(Student plays one octave higher)*

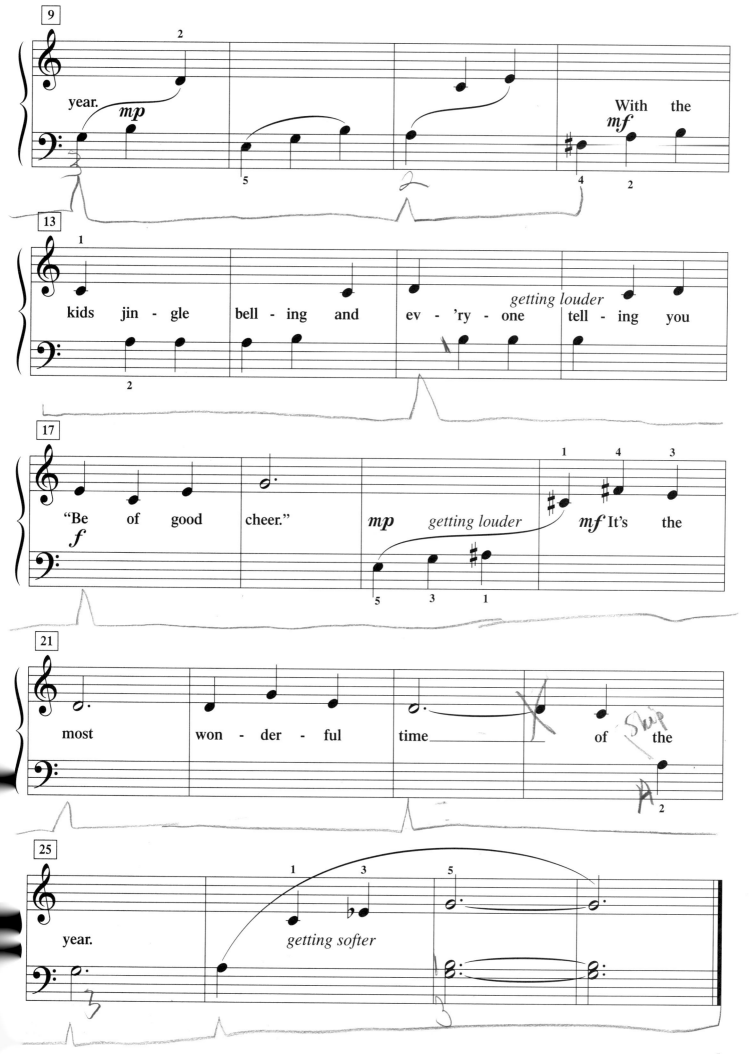

About the Pieces and Composers

Santa Claus Is Comin' to Town

This song, written at the start of America's "Great Depression," has been a source of good news for many children throughout the years with its promise that Santa would be coming soon! But it also warns the children "He's making a list, he's checking it twice, gonna find out who's naughty or nice!"

(There's No Place Like) Home for the Holidays

It was Judy Garland who said, "There's no place like home" at the end of *The Wizard of Oz*. Lyricist Al Stillman added "for the holidays" to create, along with composer Robert Allen, this Christmastime favorite. But as you will see, the song actually makes no direct references to Christmas itself. It does, however, express the universal feeling that we all want to be home for the holidays, wherever that may be! Keke Palmer sang this song in the *2007 Disney Channel Holiday* CD.

He Is Born (*Il est né*)

The music for this beautiful French carol (also known as *Born Is He*) was likely written in the eighteenth century, with the lyrics added some years later. As you prepare to play this piece, consider the lyric "play the oboe and bagpipes merrily!" You will play the part of the oboe and create the spirited melody while your teacher takes on the role of the bagpiper, 'pumping' out the chords in true bagpipe fashion.

Rudolph the Red-Nosed Reindeer

The song *Rudolph the Red-Nosed Reindeer* was inspired by a promotional comic book from a department store chain in the 1930s and has become one of the most beloved Christmas songs of all time. It was written by Johnny Marks and was first recorded by Gene Autry, the famous "Singing Cowboy" from the 1940s and 1950s. Since then, it has been recorded over 500 times and has sold an amazing 150,000,000 records!

About the Pieces and Composers

Over the River and Through the Woods

This holiday favorite was originally a poem written by Lydia Maria Child and first published in 1844 under the title "A Boy's Thanksgiving Day." Child was a novelist, journalist, and teacher who wrote extensively about the need to eliminate slavery.

In 1897, a book of carols which included this song was published and the Reverend Edward Trotter claimed authorship of the music, using the present day title. Trotter's claim is disputable as he also claimed to have written *The First Noël* and several other traditional carols included in the same collection.

Ding Dong! Merrily on High

This gentle French folk melody first appeared in a book about ballet dancing published in 1588 entitled *Orchésographie*. More than three centuries later, Englishman George Woodward added lyrics and this Christmastime favorite was born. Recently, the noted British vocalist Charlotte Church recorded this song, and in 2006 the group Celtic Woman included their version of it on their *Christmas Celebration* CD.

It's the Most Wonderful Time of the Year

You will recognize this very popular Christmas "waltz" from the many television commercials in which it has been featured. First written and recorded in 1963, it was a big hit for Andy Williams, a very popular singer from that era. In 2007, it was the sixth most played Christmas song on the radio in the United States.

ABOUT THE ARRANGERS

Edwin McLean

Edwin McLean is a composer living in Chapel Hill, North Carolina. He is a graduate of the Yale School of Music, where he studied with Krzysztof Penderecki and Jacob Druckman. He also holds a master's degree in music theory and a bachelor's degree in piano performance from the University of Colorado.

Mr. McLean has been the recipient of several grants and awards: The MacDowell Colony, the John Work Award, the Woods Chandler Prize (Yale), Meet the Composer, Florida Arts Council, and many others. He has also won the Aliénor Composition Competition for his work *Sonata for Harpsichord*, published by The FJH Music Company Inc. and recorded by Elaine Funaro (*Into the Millennium*, Gasparo GSCD-331). His complete works for harpsichord are available on the Miami Bach Society recording, *Edwin McLean: Sonatas for 1, 2, and 3 Harpsichords*. Since 1979, Edwin McLean has arranged the music of some of today's best-known recording artists. Currently, he is senior editor for The FJH Music Company Inc.

Kevin Olson

Kevin Olson is an active pianist, composer, and member of the piano faculty at Utah State University, where he teaches piano literature, pedagogy, and accompanying courses. In addition to his collegiate teaching responsibilities, Kevin directs the Utah State Youth Conservatory, which provides weekly group and private piano instruction to more than 200 pre-college, community students. The National Association of Schools of Music has recently recognized the Utah State Youth Conservatory as a model for pre-college piano instruction programs. Before teaching at Utah State, he was on the faculty at Elmhurst College near Chicago and Humboldt State University in northern California.

A native of Utah, Kevin began composing at age five. When he was twelve, his composition, *An American Trainride*, received the Overall First Prize at the 1983 National PTA Convention at Albuquerque, New Mexico. Since then he has been a Composer in Residence at the National Conference on Piano Pedagogy, and has written music commissioned and performed by groups such as the American Piano Quartet, Chicago a cappella, the Rich Matteson Jazz Festival, and several piano teacher associations around the country. He holds a Doctor of Education degree fron National-Louis University, and a bachelor's and a master's degree in music composition from Brigham Young University. Kevin maintains a large piano studio, teaching students of a variety of ages and abilities. Many of the needs of his own piano students have inspired more than 100 books and solos published by The FJH Music Company, which he joined as a writer in 1994.

USING THE CD

A great way to prepare for your Christmas recitals is to listen to the CD.

Enjoy listening to these wonderful pieces anywhere anytime! Listen to them casually (as background music) and attentively. After you have listened to the CD you might discuss interpretation with your teacher and follow along with your score as you listen.

LISTENING ACTIVITY

Listen to the CD and circle the BEST answer:

1. Circle the Christmas piece that is the most **SMOOTH:**

   Go, Tell It on the Mountain (Track 2)

   (There's No Place Like) Home for the Holidays (Track 8)

2. Which Christmas piece is in $\frac{4}{4}$ time?

   Do You Hear What I Hear? (Track 5)

   A Merry Merry Christmas to You (Track 6)

3. In which Christmas piece do you hear an **INTRODUCTION** before the melody is heard?

   Good King Wenceslas (Track 1)

   Christmas Is Coming (Track 4)

4. In which Christmas piece do you hear and play **B flats?**

   Santa Claus Is Comin' to Town (Track 7)

   He Is Born (Track 9)

5. Which Christmas piece has only ONE dynamic level?

   Go, Tell It On the Mountain (Track 2)

   Rudolph the Red-Nosed Reindeer (Track 10)

6. Which Christmas piece is in $\frac{3}{4}$ time?

   Over the River and Through the Woods (Track 11)

   Ding Dong! Merrily on High (Track 12)

Which is/are your FAVORITE Christmas piece(s)?

_____

_____

_____

_____

Answers: 1. (There's No Place Like) Home for the Holidays 2. Do You Hear What I Hear? 3. Christmas Is Coming 4. Santa Claus Is Comin' to Town 5. Go, Tell It On the Mountain 6. Over the River and Through the Woods

THE FJH PIANIST'S CURRICULUM® BY HELEN MARLAIS

IN RECITAL®

The *In Recital*® series is a fabulous and diverse collection of motivational repertoire for the early elementary to late intermediate pianist. The fine composers/arrangers of this series have created engaging original solos, duets, and arrangements of famous classical themes, jazz works, and Christmas music. This variety of genres also includes selections written for holidays throughout the year. All books include CDs with complete performances. Performance strategies and rehearsal suggestions assist with recital preparation. Designed to motivate your students with attainable goals, this comprehensively-leveled curriculum will make for phenomenal recital performances!

- **Musically engaging pieces by leading FJH composers and arrangers**

- **Original solos for recitals, contests and festivals**

- **Carefully leveled to ensure attainable goals—crucial in motivating students**

- **Recital repertoire for the entire year**

- **Solos and duets**

- **Variety of genres from classical music to jazz, blues, and rags, Christmas, popular, and all-time favorites**

- **Performance strategies and rehearsal suggestions**

Companion CD included

In Recital® Throughout the Year, Volume One

In Recital® Throughout the Year, Volume Two

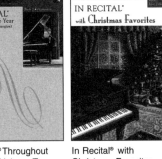
In Recital® with Christmas Favorites

In Recital® Duets

In Recital® with Classical Themes, Volume One

In Recital® with Jazz, Blues, & Rags

In Recital® with Popular Christmas Music

In Recital® with Popular Music

In Recital® with All-Time Favorites

In Recital with...

Satish Bhakta, Melody Bober, Timothy Brown, Kevin Costley, Martín Cuéllar, Lee Evans, Christopher Goldston, Elizabeth W. Greenleaf, David Karp, Nancy Lau, Mary Leaf, Chris Lobdell, Edwin McLean, Emilie Lin, Helen Marlais, Kevin Olson, Wynn-Anne Rossi, Robert Schultz, Jason Sifford, Valerie Roth Roubos, and Judith R. Strickland.

Edited, compiled, and recorded by Helen Marlais